IT WAS A BEAUTIFUL DAY
WHEN MY FATHER DIED

IT WAS A
BEAUTIFUL DAY
WHEN MY
FATHER DIED

Octavio Cesar Martinez

OCTAVIO CESAR MARTINEZ

THREE UNCLES
PUBLISHING

Published by Three Uncles Publishing
P. O. Box 150419
San Rafael, CA 94915
www.threeunclespublishing.com

ISBN: 978-0-9961251-3-0

To Octavio and Carmen,
my parents,
whom I love and miss.
Every day.

PRAISE BE TO THE GOD AND FATHER
of our LORD JESUS CHRIST,
THE FATHER OF COMPASSION AND THE
GOD OF ALL COMFORT,
WHO COMFORTS US IN ALL OUR
TROUBLES, SO THAT WE CAN COMFORT
THOSE IN ANY TROUBLE
WITH THE COMFORT WE OURSELVES
RECEIVE FROM GOD.
FOR JUST AS WE SHARE ABUNDANTLY
IN THE SUFFERINGS OF CHRIST,
SO ALSO OUR COMFORT ABOUNDS
THROUGH CHRIST.[1]

— Saint Paul

contents

Acknowledgements

There are many people who have contributed to or spoken into my life. To the best of my ability, I've listed a few in alphabetical order: Michael Adnoff, Dr. Edward "Chip" Anderson, Dr. Eric Bryant, Dr. Thomas M. Crisp, Alex Gilbert, Janine Goldsmith-Ripley, Dr. David Gonzalez, Joby Harris, John Huffman, Jean-Marie Jobs, John Om, John Puls, Janice Sakuma, Steve Sakuma, Cory Shaw, Lisa Shaw, Dr. Gregg Ten Elshof, Tom Taylor, Barbara Wood, and most of all, Rick Yamamoto, my friend, mentor and travel companion.

Anything good in my life is the result of these men and women.

Mistakes are all mine.

Thanks to everyone who attended Sojourn and Mosaic Whittier.

It was my privilege and pleasure to have been your pastor.

Unforgettable

The first beating I recall rocked the hell out of me.

He crashed his fist into my jaw with such force that it knocked me off my feet. I would have collapsed, but he held me up by my shirt. Before I could process what happened, I was hit again. And again. And again. I tried to stop this humiliation by holding up my hands. That was a futile attempt to defend myself. He was stronger, and taller, and trained as a boxer. I was outmatched.

I saw his giant fist coming at my jaw. He had the thick meaty fingers of a man who had worked with his hands all his life. But the most vivid thing I recall is his gold pinky ring. It was custom made— a simple gold ring with his initials: OGM.

One blow landed on my rib cage. It took the air out of me. I couldn't breathe for a few seconds, so I didn't cry. My face felt hot. My ears were ringing. But when I was able to breathe again, then I did start to cry.

He stopped.

He let go of my shirt.

I was winded and I hurt all over.

My knees buckled and I fell down.

I noticed a button was torn off my shirt
and another was undone.

I pulled myself up and stumbled to bed.

He straightened up and walked away.

He was 34.

I was 7.

He was my father.

I was his son.

And it was a beautiful day when my father died.

Chapter One

IN AMERICA

THE WORLD IS A BOOK, AND THOSE WHO DO NOT TRAVEL READ ONLY ONE PAGE.[2]

— *Saint Augustine*

My parents arrived in America as illegal immigrants. If you believe America isn't friendly to Hispanic immigrants now, imagine what it was like in the 1950s. Also imagine leaving your home, your family, your culture, and your country. Why did my parents come to America? Like all immigrants before and since: for a better life. In Durango, DGO., Mexico, my mother was a beautician and my father was a manual laborer.

In America, my father went to work in a kitchen. He washed dishes, cleaned pots and pans, and eventually became a cook. He learned how to butcher meats, create desserts, make soups, sauces and salads. It was his creative outlet and he was good at it. My mother went to work in a sewing factory making clothes. The *fabrica*, she called it. Nine months and ten days after they were married, my sister Dora Luz was born. My mother had two miscarriages, then I was born, then three years later, my brother Cesar Onesimo arrived. My parents knew no other life than working and raising kids.

We grew up in Huntington Park, a white suburban neighborhood of Los Angeles in a rented one-bedroom bungalow on Belgrave Avenue. In 1965, my parents bought their home at 6613 Malabar St. Life was good. My parents had made it. The American dream: a two-car garage, a front yard and backyard, three bedrooms, one bathroom, and only two blocks away from the elementary school we walked to each morning.

On Saturday mornings my sister, brother, and I would walk the mile to St. Matthias church for catechism. It was good moral training for us and a few hours of peace and quiet for my mother and father. Each Saturday was also a working day. Once we arrived home from catechism, we had chores to do around the house. My mother, sister, and younger brother did inside work. My father and I would do outside work. Fixing fences, cutting bushes, mowing the lawn, or painting. There was always something to do to keep the house in tiptop condition. I learned about tools and house maintenance from my father, but I really wanted to stay inside; housework seemed more attractive to me. The dusting, the mopping, laundry, whatever my mom, sister, and brother did, seemed to be more fun than being outside.

As Catholics, we attended mass on Sundays; celebrated birthdays, Thanksgivings, Christmases, and every other holiday. My mother would often cook meals that we would eat outside on our patio. And because we are Mexican, we had a lemon tree. Normal meals were typical 1960s American dinners (salad, potatoes, some meat, and Kool-Aid to drink), but sometimes my mother would make a delicious Mexican meal. She was a fantastic cook. Caldos (soup), beef tongue, menudo, tacos, and my favorite at the time, *tacos de cessos* (cow brains). We sat at a round wooden table. If we were not eating outside, we ate in the kitchen. I cannot recall a single time we ate in the dining room. And, we had to finish everything we were served. No matter what. No matter how long it took. Once I recall sitting for over an hour trying to finish some cold, dry meal my mother had prepared, but I learned a trick: sprinkle a little sugar on the food that had become cold and tasteless, to make it easier to eat.

In America, my parents bought a home, worked, raised a family, made love, celebrated, wept, fought, dreamed, died and were buried. In America, my father drank, beat us, and left my mother for another woman.

Chapter Two

JULY 2, 2004

HOMO HOMINI LUPUS.[3]

— Plautus

He died on July 2, 2004. It was the kind of day
people move to Los Angeles for: blue skies,
low humidity, big clouds, a cool breeze from the
west, temperature in the low 70s.

My father and I are twins separated by 27 years.
We have similar mannerisms, height, hair,
appearance, personality, and love of clothes, food,
and music. Our upbringings were different;
I grew up middle class in America, and he grew
up poor in Mexico.

On the way to finding out who he was, I discovered
that he was an amateur boxing champ, a lumberjack,
a miner, and who knows what else as he drifted
through his young adult years. Most people would
know him as a successful French sous-chef.
As an illegal immigrant in the early 50s, he started
in the restaurant industry as a dishwasher long

before he became a sous-chef. Later, he would go on to cook for two U.S. presidents, the king of Sweden, the Rolling Stones, and other celebrities. Numerous hotels and restaurants wanted him in their kitchens.

He possessed that easy way of making friends— everywhere and with everyone. He dressed well, he loved dancing, and he always smelled good. My father was affectionate, creative, funny, kind, and often gave good advice. He was also generous. And I don't mean sort of generous—I mean shirt-off-his-back generous. He would give away his tools, money, time, and his love. Younger men wanted him to be their father. My father was well-liked, and I loved him.

About every two years he'd buy a brand new GM Pontiac. During that same year our family would take that gas-guzzling, American-made beast of a machine across the 10 East and hang a right at El Paso to visit *familia* in Mexico. That's a Mexican vacation: you go home *para ver la familia*.

My mother would gather clothes, sugar-free gum, and over-the-counter medicines to give to her family.

My father (who by this time had become a U.S. citizen) smuggled handguns and rifles into Mexico. Once I was told to pretend to be asleep on top of a few rifles to prevent the family car from being searched. He also carried cash (American dollars) and Marlboro cigarettes to pay the *mordidas* (bribes) to Mexican law enforcement officials.

My father was many things to many people, but I remembered him as a AAA dad—alcoholic, abuser, adulterer—all of this stingingly crossed my threshold and I hated him.

I had been on the business end of his beatings more than once. On at least two occasions, I went to school with visible bruises and bandages. I thought what an awful thing I must be that my own father would beat me. But years later I understood: there's nothing a skinny boy could do to deserve a beating dealt out by a grown man. Even now,

I can see his left fist coming at my jaw. And even now I can see his angry face. Who deserves that memory? I was afraid of him.

Physical wounds are one thing. They're easy to deal with. You can treat them, you can ice them, you can bandage them, and in time they'll heal. But the unseen wounds are a real bitch. Like little black holes sucking all the light and life out of your soul until they finally consume you.

Consume you completely.

Your heart.

Your soul.

Your mind.

Bitterness, anger, unforgiveness—they suffocated my ability to give or experience love in any healthy way. And it left me a walking corpse trying to breathe. And that was only part of the problem. Hurt is not sustainable. My hurt morphed into anger. And then my anger morphed into contempt. And that is where I held my father for many years. In contempt.

Past the hurt.

Past the anger.

I held him in contempt.

For years.

When my father died, it was a beautiful day in Los Angeles.

It was July 2, 2004.

Chapter Three

I'M SORRY FOR YOUR LOSS

BUT WHEN THAT SERVANT WENT
OUT, HE FOUND ONE OF HIS
FELLOW SERVANTS WHO OWED
HIM A HUNDRED SILVER COINS.
HE GRABBED HIM AND BEGAN
TO CHOKE HIM. "PAY BACK WHAT
YOU OWE ME!" HE DEMANDED.

HIS FELLOW SERVANT FELL
TO HIS KNEES AND BEGGED HIM,
"BE PATIENT WITH ME, AND
I WILL PAY IT BACK." BUT HE
REFUSED. INSTEAD, HE WENT OFF
AND HAD THE MAN THROWN
INTO PRISON UNTIL HE COULD
PAY THE DEBT.[4]   —*Jesus of Nazareth*

As a former Police Chaplain, I completed both
a civilian academy and the L.A. County
Sheriff's department training, which included:
fingerprinting, handling forensic evidence,
and shooting three types of firearms: a shotgun,
an M6 semi-automatic rifle, and a 9mm pistol.

I became competent in all three. Chaplains wore bullet proof (read, resistant) vests. Our uniform was a navy polo with a sewn LASD badge, and dark slacks; we also wore a dark navy windbreaker with CLERGY emblazoned in large yellow sans-serif font on our backs. That way, hopefully, no one would shoot us.

Chaplains have several responsibilities, but the one job every chaplain hates is death notifications. Chaplains are often called on to perform a death notification. Too often. And a death notification is exactly what it sounds like: you notify a victim's family that the deceased is, well, deceased.

Death notifications are awful. They take so long. And they take so long because law enforcement officials must make sure they are notifying the right person about the right person. And while this is going on, the victim's family is in a state of high anxiety, wondering what has happened to their loved one. When a law enforcement officer shows up at your door with a partner, and that partner is wearing little crosses on the shirt collar, that's a chaplain. And it's never good news when a chaplain shows up.

After we made sure we were talking to the right party, the deputy or officer would say to us, "Chaplain…" and that was our cue. I learned to get to the point. I learned not to speak of death in euphemisms (e.g., passed away, is no longer with us), and just say it: "Your son / daughter / father / mom has died. I'm sorry for your loss." Often, I would also weep with the victim's family.

When my brother called me around 2:00 p.m. on that Friday afternoon in July 2004, to say our father had died, I replied, "I'm sorry for your loss."

His loss.

Not my loss.

After discussing a few details, we hung up. I looked up at the sky. "What a beautiful day," I thought, and I went back into my home. Back to

working on a sermon. No emotion. No hesitation.
No interruption. I would have had a bigger
response if my brother had told me the McRib was
back. By the time of my father's physical death,
my father had already been dead to me for many years,
so his actual death meant little.

On July 7th, 2004, I officiated my father's funeral.
It was like other funerals I had officiated before
and since: there's a deceased, there's a coffin,
and there are friends and family members in various
states of grief and disbelief. Often, I would be
so affected by their grief, I would weep. My father's
funeral was a carbon copy except for one thing:
I didn't care at all.

No emotion.

None.

My dad's actions—everything he was—completely,
and absolutely dulled my heart to him. My emotional
energy was needed and better spent elsewhere in
my busy life, than on him. I settled for not giving a

damn, which ended up closing down an important part of my heart (which I will always need).
But you can never choke off only a "part" of your heart. Eventually, all of it dies. Slowly, but it dies.

While he was in the hospital, he asked to see me. I didn't go. Keep in mind, as a pastor or chaplain, hospital visits are part of the deal. You get a call, you go. Any hour of day or night. You go. But I didn't go see my father as he lay on his death bed. I didn't want to go. As far as I knew then, he died alone, and I didn't care.

At my father's funeral, people came to me and offered their condolences. Grown men with moist eyes would tell me all the ways my father had helped them get jobs, restore relationships... on and on it went. Aunts, uncles, cousins from Mexico were there. Local family were there too. They shared their favorite memories of my father. Each one would break down, experience grief, and weep. And when they did, I did what I had done many times before.

But this time I felt nothing. I replied:

"I'm sorry for your loss."

Chapter Four

SUMMER OF 1979

GET RID OF ALL BITTERNESS,
RAGE AND ANGER, BRAWLING
AND SLANDER, ALONG WITH
EVERY FORM OF MALICE.
BE KIND AND COMPASSIONATE
TO ONE ANOTHER, FORGIVING
EACH OTHER, JUST AS IN CHRIST
GOD FORGAVE YOU.[5] — *Saint Paul*

I have an older sister and a younger brother and a
mother and father. We lived a comfortable
middle class life. From what I could tell, of all my
friends, we had the biggest and best looking home,
and my parents were better looking than any
other set of parents my friends had. I had my own
bed, never went hungry, wore clean clothes,
and went to the doctor and dentist regularly.

My father always had a job. He always worked.
He worked hard at his job and he worked hard in
his home.

Our family ate together most nights. And my mom
was a great cook. Sometimes we ate Mexican
food but often we had traditional American meals.
But even though my father was a chef, he
rarely cooked at home because as he often said,
"This is not my kitchen." On occasion, my
parents would take us out to eat. And that meant
Mexican food in East Los Angeles, or KFC or
Burger King, or tacos from spots my father knew.

My mom grew up in the era when women always
dressed, always did their makeup even if they
were just at home. And she smoked in the elegant
manner of women of the 1960s. She also
wore the hell out of Jean Naté After Bath Splash
by Revlon.

My father was always well-groomed. He shaved
every day, wore fitted clothing, and combed
his hair in a classic side part with short side burns.
He would dress for work, change into his chef
whites, then change back into his dress clothes for

the drive home. I never saw my father wear jeans
or tennis shoes.

Not once.

Ever.

My parents raised me, my sister, and my brother
in a typical middle class manner. Our parents
gave us housing, food, education, and the security
of an intact family consisting of one father,
one mother, and the occasional pet. But most
families have a dark side hidden from public view.
We had ours. And in our family it was one of
alcoholism and domestic violence.

When I was in my 20s, my father left my mother for
a woman who was 15 years younger than my mom.
When my father left my mom, he left us all,
but I felt as if he left me most of all. I wasn't able to
help anyone the night he left. I was too
wrapped up in my own feelings to be of any comfort
to my mother. I didn't call my sister or brother.

I wept that night. I wondered why he didn't love me enough to stay.

I was 21.

My father was 48.

I was starting a marriage.

He was ending one.

It was the summer of 1979.

Chapter Five

HE PRAYED WITH OPEN EYES:

OCTAVIO GONZALEZ MARTINEZ - I

…FOR I, THE LORD YOUR GOD…(PUNISH) THE CHILDREN FOR THE SIN OF THE PARENTS TO THE THIRD AND FOURTH GENERATION OF THOSE WHO HATE ME.[6]

— Exodus 20

I have many memories of my father. One of the earliest and clearest is the one I am most unsure of. I am not certain if I'm remembering the event or if I am recalling a 8mm home movie of the same event. My father is wearing a navy suit, white shirt, and red tie. He is young, clean-shaven, and holding my newborn baby brother, Cesar, who is about three years younger than me. They had just brought him home from the hospital. It was August 1960.

I can recall my dad playing "horsey" with me. He taught me to respect firearms, policemen, doctors, and teachers. To stand when an elder entered the room. To give up my seat to people who were disabled or blind. Driving through Los Angeles, he would point out people who lived on the street or under freeway overpasses, shaking his head and saying, "That's bad," in his heavily-accented English. From that alone, I understood we were fortunate to have a home to go to, a bed to sleep in, and food to eat. My parents provided that.

As a sous-chef, he worked nights, weekends, various parties, and every holiday, Thanksgiving and Christmas included. He cooked for dignitaries, celebrities, and politicians. Whenever he was cooking for a domestic or foreign leader, FBI agents and Secret Service agents would clear the kitchen staff before the event. And those agents hovered in the kitchen, shadowing the staff as they cooked and prepared the dinners.

When he came home from those events, I'd ask what he made for these important people and he would proudly describe the food. A duck dish, a soufflé, a fancy dessert. It sounded so exotic and interesting.

One night, he had to cook for the King of Sweden.
When he arrived home to kiss us goodnight,
I noticed he was still wearing his chef whites. I put
my arm around his neck and felt his cold
wet jacket. Wet from sweat. Cold because he was
no longer in a hot kitchen. As always, I asked
what he made: "Popi, what did the King eat?"

His reply? "The shit I made him."

It must have been a rough event.

As I mentioned, he was always clean-shaven
and grew a mustache in his later years. A big ol'
Pancho Villa special. He wore the hell out
of English Leather and in his later years, Aramis.

Always clean.

Always neat.

So I always thought: this is what a man does.
This is how a man dresses.

You work outside of your home, you buy

American-made cars, you drink Budweiser at lunch,
you're funny, and you're always well-groomed.

I recall his prayers. Actually, I never heard him pray.
I'd see him pray. My father was raised Methodist,
but converted to Catholicism to marry my mother.
He took few things seriously, but two were
church and God.

I loved (and still love) the Catholic Church.
The church with all of its majesty and mystery: the
smell of incense, the sounds shoes made on the
marbled floors, the art, the feel of the wood, and the
sounds of my smock as I walked.

And I learned to take it seriously because of
my father.

He was so strong. So big in my eyes. So when
he kneeled and prayed, I noticed. Who was God,
that my dad would bend his knee and pray
to Him? What did my dad know that I did not?
I can see his face, the profile of his face as he prayed.
His eyes darting back and forth. Never closed.

Always open when he prayed. And he prayed silently to himself. So I never heard my father pray.

I'd see his lips move. With his eyes open, looking up, looking back and forth.

And I wonder if he ever found what he was looking for.

Chapter Six

HE WAS SEVEN WHEN HIS MOTHER TRIED TO HANG HIM:

OCTAVIO GONZALEZ MARTINEZ - 11

...BUT SHOWING LOVE TO A THOUSAND GENERATIONS

OF THOSE WHO LOVE ME AND KEEP MY COMMANDMENTS.[7]

— Exodus 20

My father was seven years old when his mother,
my grandmother, tried to hang him. He was about
nine years old when his father, my grandfather,
said he could no longer sleep with him in the same
bed. I heard these two stories from my dad
when I was about eight or nine years old. And for
him, they were connected. I don't believe he
knew why. I was in my early teens when my dad told
me more about his mom, my grandmother.
I only ever saw one black and white photo of her:
she's in her early 30s, deep dark eyes, her black
shiny hair pulled back into a bun. Her lips appear
full, her skin flawless, and she wore a floral
printed dress with a high collar.

I never knew her in real life. I never saw her. I never heard her voice. But clearly, he remembered her.

He said she was a no-nonsense, humorless, strict kind of woman. And one day, my dad discovered how strict, humorless, and no nonsense she could be. While I do not recall all the elements of the story, I remember my dad said he was tied up, hands behind his back, placed on a stool with a noose around his neck. And he recalled when his father, my grandfather, came home unexpectedly and rescued him. But, and this is the point of the story, he was never sure if she was really going to hang him or not.

His mother, my grandmother, died not long after that. In grief, my dad, a small boy, took comfort sleeping in his father's bed. This went on for a few months. Then my grandfather remarried and sleeping with dad was no longer an option. My dad almost winced at this part of the story, recalling how it hurt to feel rejected by his father. As a grown man, he understood why he had to move out of his dad's bedroom. But as a small boy who lost his mother, it must have felt like he lost his father too.

At his mother's funeral, he and his older brother, Armando, cut a piece of wood off their mother's coffin. My father kept his piece of wood for years. He had fashioned the wood pieces into a small cross, which he placed in a gold medallion on a gold chain which my father wore around his neck.

But in over 65 years, he never got over the loss of his mother or what his father's rejection felt like to him, a small nine-year-old boy.

Chapter Seven

THE BIBLE CHANGES NO ONE AND LOVE DOESN'T REDEEM

I HAVE FORESWORN MYSELF.
I HAVE BROKEN EVERY LAW I
HAVE SWORN TO UPHOLD,
I HAVE BECOME WHAT I BEHELD
AND I AM CONTENT THAT I HAVE
DONE RIGHT![8] — *Eliot Ness, The Untouchables*

SO I FIND THIS LAW AT WORK:
ALTHOUGH I WANT TO DO
GOOD, EVIL IS RIGHT THERE
WITH ME. FOR IN MY INNER
BEING I DELIGHT IN GOD'S LAW;
BUT I SEE ANOTHER LAW AT
WORK IN ME, WAGING WAR
AGAINST THE LAW OF MY MIND
AND MAKING ME A PRISONER
OF THE LAW OF SIN AT WORK
WITHIN ME.[9]   — *Saint Paul*

So this is where I come clean.

Well, cleaner.

My 20s were a decade of violence. I became my dad.
I was on my way to becoming violent long before
I was an adult. In elementary school, I had stabbed
two classmates: one in the back and the other
in the butt. Both times my weapon of choice was a
sharpened No. 2 pencil. I don't think I was yet 10.

I hurt animals, myself, and others. Sometimes
with my fists. Once in a fight with a bigger kid,
I struck him with a hand-sized rock across
the face. Fight over.

In junior high school, I enrolled in martial arts.
I learned to throw a punch correctly, how to
pivot my feet and position my wrist so I would not
break my hand—a lesson I forgot in my 20s.
Then I gained a reputation which carried me
through high school without one fight. But I wasn't
above getting into a street fight. I learned anger
and adrenaline could give you a distinct advantage in

most fights.

I recall one event when I tried to drag a driver out of his car. There were three other men in the car, too. But in hindsight, if a skinny, long-haired, army-trench-coat-wearing lunatic is beating down the glass of your car window with his bloody fists, you'd probably think better than to open the door. By the way, the glass didn't break (Damn you, safety glass. Damn you to hell!).

I recall a gas station in Pasadena where I hurled a tire at someone who tried my (lack of) patience. Then there was the group of four Asian teenagers I picked a fight with… okay, that one I lost big time. Then there were the three Mexican gang bangers who flipped me off. I chased them in my yellow cream Toyota Corolla. Did I mention my wife was in the car? Oh wait, did I mention my two small sons were in the car… strapped in their car seats? In that case, Providence intervened and I stopped myself from pursuing those punks.

I had run-ins with the police, and strangers.
More than once my temper and lack of control got
me into hot water. What I remember the most
from those days was the feeling of being trapped.
I wanted to change. I couldn't change. I brought
years of pent-up fear, anger, and violence into my
adulthood and marriage.

And I was active in church all the while.

I attended Bible study and church services about two
or three times a week. I taught a Bible study class.
I knew I wasn't right. I knew something was wrong,
but I was too proud to ask for help. I didn't know
who to ask.

Finally, after one particularly ugly act of violence,
I came clean to a friend from church. Michael.
He didn't judge. He didn't coddle, either. He was
direct and helped me get well.

I have not wasted that gift.

Chapter Eight

THE 80s AND THAT F'n BIRD

THERE IS FAR MORE TO YOUR
LIFE THAN THE FOOD YOU PUT
IN YOUR STOMACH, MORE TO
YOUR OUTER APPEARANCE THAN
THE CLOTHES YOU HANG ON
YOUR BODY. LOOK AT THE
BIRDS, FREE AND UNFETTERED,
NOT TIED DOWN TO A JOB
DESCRIPTION, CARELESS IN THE
CARE OF GOD. AND YOU COUNT
FAR MORE TO HIM THAN BIRDS.[10]

—*Jesus of Nazareth*

When your soul is sick and broken, even the sacred
can be used to hurt others. Even the sacred
can be used for evil, for darkness. You can use holy
writings to hate another person. A twisted,
hateful person will use the holy words in twisted,
hateful ways. And I was twisted by hate.
After the initial shock of my father leaving my

mother, I tried to connect with my father.
But goodness he made it difficult.

He always seemed to have an excuse to not be
present at events I invited him to. There is a
ball park one—ONE—block from the house where
my father used to live with his second wife.
My sons played baseball or practiced baseball many
times at that park. I invited him to their games
and practices often. He never came. Too busy or who
knows what, but he would show up unexpectedly
at my home. So I learned to take what I was given.

In my late 20s, life had settled into a routine: eat,
work, sleep, kids, church, house errands and repeat.
Over and over. For years. Often I would work
two jobs to make ends meet. There was one year that
I worked; I mean I worked the entire year.
No days off. A light day meant only working one job
instead of two. But I was young, and had a
small family to provide for. You do what you have
to do. It was what it was. Still, sometimes, I did
not make ends meet.

December is big in retail. Huge. But come January, after the post-Christmas sales end, there's February. The absolute worst month in retail. And for commissioned sales reps, it's a nightmare. So it happened. I came up short for the rent. I was embarrassed. Who would I ask? Who would help me? I was not looking for a gift; I needed a loan. So after a while thinking over my options, I called my father. And within a few moments, he agreed to loan me the three hundred dollars I was short. I agreed to pay him back within four months. March rent would be covered. Big relief. Big load off my mind. I'm good. Yes, my father is going to help me.

Then two weeks went by. I called to get the money he promised me.

"You know, Tavo, Sonia and I were talking it over… and I'm not going to lend you the money."

"What the hell? Are you kidding me?" I thought.

I wasn't mad. I wasn't angry. I felt too hurt for that.

It was yet another dismissal from my father.
And by the way, he had every right to say he could
not or would not lend me the money, but to
not tell me until the last minute—that's what hurt.
I could have had time to work extra hours, sell
something… anything to make the money I needed.
But no, he didn't think about that. He didn't
think about how breaking his promise would affect
others. This was my moment of clarity. It was
then I recall thinking: "I don't have a father."

I know, I know… a little dramatic. But I realized
I did not have a father, a mature man, a wise man, to
guide me or to rely on. I had my dad as my father.
A man who would break his promises to his family
when it suited him. And it suited him to break
his promise to me.

I swallowed my pride, and I called a friend
from church who immediately offered to help. I paid
the rent, and two months later I made good with
him for the loan. But two weeks—TWO—weeks
after my father said he would not lend me the

money for the rent, my family and I were at his home for a visit. And then my dad said, "Let me show you the bird I bought."

My father was so self-absorbed that he didn't think about how I would feel about this. You see, he told me he bought this cockatoo, that f'n bird, the day after he promised to lend his son money to cover the rent. How much did that bird cost? You guessed it. The same amount he promised to lend me. It was a punch in my gut. I mattered less than a bird to my father.

Jesus taught His early followers that God provides for even the birds. He also taught them that they matter much more than those birds to the Father in heaven who feeds them. But to my father on earth, I mattered less than a bird. Hurt morphed into anger, now disrespect. This f'n bird is more important than I am to him.

And that moment was the tipping point.

And the turning point.

I would no longer connect to my piece-of-shit dad.

"After all the shit you put our family through,"
I thought to myself—

"The drinking, the fighting,

beating me up, hitting my mother,

the affair, and now this shit?

I will never ask you for help.

You and I are done.

You're dead to me."

And now, I had a new place for my father. A place called contempt. And in contempt I would lock him up, and forget him. After all, he was a man who would cheat on his wife. And his new wife was a woman who would seduce a married man.

They deserved each other.

So f' you and that f'n bird too.

Chapter Nine

SUMMER OF 2003

AND WHEN YOU STAND PRAYING, IF YOU HOLD ANYTHING AGAINST ANYONE, FORGIVE THEM, SO THAT YOUR FATHER IN HEAVEN MAY FORGIVE YOU YOUR SINS.[11]

—Jesus of Nazareth

All my adult children have a genetic condition.
Each one has it worse than their older sibling.
My second son spent some time in a hospital for
surgery to correct what the disease had done
to his body. The expected two-to-three-day hospital
stay lasted one week, then a second week, and
a third seemed possible. My wife and I decided to
respect and protect our son's privacy and we
told no one about his condition.

Day after day, we went to spend time at the hospital
as he recovered. Every night after work, we
would drive in traffic to see him. He did not look
good. Already thin, he was losing more weight,

losing his color, and losing his personality. Still, we kept the situation to ourselves and did not share it with anyone.

Except my brother.

My younger brother was closer to my dad than I was. At least I thought they were closer.
My brother spoke with my father more often than I spoke to him. Turns out, my brother, who had more money than I had, often bailed out my dad.
My brother shared the condition of my son, his nephew, with my dad. My son's grandfather.
And then my father called me.

I reluctantly answered the phone.

"Yes, Popi?"

"I just heard about Mike. What happened?"

"Nothing, Pops, he's going to be okay," I replied, my annoyance growing.

"Yes, but you should have told someone. You should

have told me."

"I didn't want to worry anyone, Pops," I countered.

"But Tavo, family is important…"

I didn't hear what he said after that. I lost it and
vomited up all my anger.

"Family is important? Are you f'n kidding me with
this shit? You f'n beat me, and Mommy, and
you were a f'n pain in my ass for years! You never
could find the time to spend one f'ing hour
to see your grandsons play baseball. They would
have loved to see you watch them. And besides
all that bullshit, you couldn't keep your pants on!"

I was yelling at that point. And I hung up on him.

A few weeks later, I received a handwritten letter
from my father. I immediately recognized
the writing. And the kind of pen he used. It was a
fountain pen. Blue ink. The pen he also used
to write down notes, and recipes. In his letter, he
apologized for everything. I mean everything.

He owned the mess he had caused, the problems
he created. And he finished the letter by asking
for forgiveness.

Here's the sick part—I knew I was beating him
up emotionally. And I liked it.

He had beaten the shit out of me years before.

I took advantage of him and turned the tables.

Now I was bigger, taller, and trained to help people.

I used that to hurt him.

When I finished reading the letter, I tore it
in half, threw it in the trash can, and said to myself,
"Too little, too late."

It was the Summer of 2003.

Chapter Ten

CANCER

MAKE A CLEAN BREAK WITH ALL
CUTTING, BACKBITING, PROFANE
TALK. BE GENTLE WITH ONE
ANOTHER, SENSITIVE. FORGIVE
ONE ANOTHER AS QUICKLY
AND THOROUGHLY AS GOD IN
CHRIST FORGAVE YOU.[12]

— *Saint Paul*

Hippocrates used the Greek term for crab to describe
cancer. Later, a Roman physician named Aulus
Cornelius Celsus translated that Greek term into
the word "cancer," the Latin term for crab.
And cancer, just like a crab, generally is not detected
until it's too late. So the word crab is the perfect
word to describe that horrible disease.

Sometimes cancer patients are misdiagnosed; their
cancers are thought to be pulled muscles, upset
stomachs, or respiratory infections. Often enough,
after the right tests, the cancer is properly diagnosed

and the right treatment is given: chemo, radiation, surgery, or a combination of the three.

My father died of a cancer that metastasized throughout his abdominal core. I was dying of a cancer that metastasized throughout the core of my being.

My heart.

My mind.

My soul.

Unforgiveness is mental, emotional, spiritual cancer. Forgiveness is the cure. Like surgery without anesthesia, it's painful. But when it's over, you're free. And alive.

After I forgave my father, I saw his humanity. Everything—and I mean everything—changed. I saw him as the nine-year-old boy who lost his mom; the man who longed for his father to love him; the young adult working to support his young family. I saw his beauty, his talents, his generosity, and remembered his laughter. I saw the frustration he experienced in his life. And I saw that I was no better than him.

In some ways, I was worse.

He was my father.

I was his son.

When I forgave him, I started to live.

Mi Familia

*My dad about 28 years old, sporting a classic side part
haircut, black plastic glasses, white t-shirt and khakis.
Me, about 6 months and my sister, Dora, about 4 years.
Circa 1958*

11 years old, leaving Mass, St Mathias, Huntington Park, CA. Circa 1968. Even now, I still wear a sport coat, or suit with tie and pocket square to Mass.

*Maria Del Carmen Hernandez, about 18 years old.
Circa 1940s. My mother was a classic beauty who always
looked and smelled put together.*

Carmen Hernandez Martinez, about 50 years old.
Circa 1980s. My mother was a strong and warm woman;
you always knew where you stood with her.

Dressing for Mass, Durango Mexico, 1969. Dora in short skirt, Mom in a dress and my dad in a suit, with a "presidential fold" pocket square. Learned my sense of style from him.

Dad took me to a TV event to meet some celebrities.
This is a photo booth picture. Los Angeles, 1961.

*My mother and me, 1957. Behind us is my parents'
wedding photo. My parents lost two girls before I was born;
she was probably happy to see I made it.*

Me, Dad, and my brother Cesar, after Mass, in Durango, Mexico, 1969. I recall loving my suede buck shoes.

My sons, Michael John and David Octavio. Glad to have seen them grow up, marry so well and begin their own families.

Chapter Eleven

ONE STAB WOUND TIMES SEVENTY-SEVEN

PETER CAME TO JESUS
AND ASKED, "LORD, HOW
MANY TIMES SHALL I FORGIVE
MY BROTHER OR SISTER WHO
SINS AGAINST ME? UP TO
SEVEN TIMES?"

JESUS ANSWERED, "I TELL
YOU, NOT SEVEN TIMES,
BUT SEVENTY-SEVEN TIMES."[13]

— *From the gospel of St. Matthew*

I have already mentioned I was a chaplain with two different police agencies. I have mentioned some of the duties we perform. One thing we also do is see. We see people at their worst. Sometimes alive. Sometimes dead. Sometimes, a victim dies right in front of you.

Death is never like the movies. It's never elegant, or noble. Victims do not have control over the timing of their deaths. They are rarely cognizant and don't "wait" for someone to be there to tell them something important before they die. When folks die, their color immediately changes; they may gurgle, foam at the mouth, yell, or quietly pass, and their eyes may roll up and out as they die.

I've seen battered bodies, crushed bodies, overdose victims, shooting and stabbing victims. But of all the kind of wounds I've seen, what stuck in my mind were stab wounds. Stabbings became, for me, the key to understanding the meaning of what Jesus said to Peter about forgiveness.

When a victim is stabbed, that one single wound may cause multiple injuries. The skin is torn open, a muscle may be cut, a bone chipped, a vein nicked, a nerve severed, and an organ punctured. All these injuries from one cut. Multiple stabbings and you can see why people can easily bleed out and die.

When I was willing to forgive my dad, I didn't just

forgive him. I FORGAVE him. For everything.
And after that powerful encounter with Divinity,
I was free on levels I did not know existed
in me. Forgiveness is often not one and done. What
I didn't know was that many of those moments
and incidents of physical and verbal abuse from my
father were emotional stab wounds.

There were many other places of injury in my heart,
my mind, and my soul that needed healing. At first
I was surprised to see that something was
left over, some residual anger or fear or hatred, even.
Gently but firmly, a close friend named Jean-Marie
was able to help me understand that forgiveness
comes on multiple levels. Then I understood what
Jesus has to say about forgiveness.

In the West we think differently than our counter-
parts in the Middle East. We are recipients
of Greek thinking. And that thinking is linear,
chronological, sequential. But not so much in the
Middle East where Jesus taught and where
our Sacred Book was written. The culture influenced

the tone and tenor of the writings in that Sacred Book. Now I understand that the seventy-seven times may be from one injury that goes deep, deep into our souls.

It's not multiple acts that need to be forgiven— it may be one huge act that has caused layers of harm to our soul. Forgiveness is like peeling an onion. Some layers may not cause a strong reaction, and other layers make you cry.

But now that I had experienced and known the freedom of forgiveness, I was not about to retreat back into bitterness. I forgave my father every time a new memory of injury surfaced. I forgave him quicker and quicker each time. And when I did I felt freer, lighter, and more grateful for the forgiveness that God had shown me.

How many times should you forgive someone?

As often as you need to.

77 seems reasonable.

Chapter Twelve

JULY 7TH, 2004

When The violin
Can forgive the past

It starts singing.

When the violin can stop worrying
About the future

You will become
Such a drunk laughing nuisance

That God
Will then lean down
And start combing you into
His Hair.

When the violin can forgive
Every wound caused by Others
The heart starts
Singing.[14]   — *Hafiz*

From the 80s to the summer of 2003—those
years passed without me reaching out to my father.
If there was contact between us, he initiated it.
I didn't call him on his birthday, didn't acknowledge
him on Father's Day, I do not think I ever
gave him a gift for Christmas. The years of hurt had
changed smoothly from anger, to disrespect,
and finally, to contempt. Or think of it as spiritual
and emotional constipation.

My father died on July 2nd; July 7th was the funeral.
Though I was asked to officiate his service,
I was not supposed to be there. I don't mean I was in
denial. Hell, I didn't care about his passing.
I wasn't supposed to be there. I was supposed to be
in New York City.

July 7th was my 25th wedding anniversary.

My wife and I lived…. how do I put this…
on a budget. She was home the first eighteen years of
our marriage. When she went to work outside
the home, it almost doubled our income overnight.

Wow, we could splurge on things here and there.

A few years rolled by and our 25th wedding anniversary was coming up. Our kids were adults.

They had jobs. An idea crossed our minds for the first time… we could take an actual vacation!

Now I had worked for the phone company for almost thirty years. I received vacation time, but to be honest, it was really more like time off with pay. My family and I would fix things around the house, go to the beach, maybe a matinée for the kids (okay, I did cry at the end of *Beauty and the Beast*), but never did we go on a vacation.

But your 25th wedding anniversary is a milestone. And now that my wife was working, we could actually afford to buy a plane ticket and go somewhere.

Not this time.

You see, my father who never managed anything well, never managed his finances either.

When he died, he and his wife had no money to

bury him. He left nothing behind, so it fell on
my brother, my sister, and me to pay for his funeral
and cremation. The three of us split the cost.
My share? Every penny we had set aside for our
first real vacation to celebrate our 25th wedding
anniversary.

I despised him at that moment. There he was, dead
in his box. A box I paid for one third of.
And there I was officiating his funeral. To honor
him. His first son. The son who bears his name.
I didn't have one good thing to say about him.
I spoke of God's love for people. I spoke of how
He freely forgives. And while I spoke, people listened.
Their heads followed my movements as
I moved across the stage. But I was unmoved.

When I finished, I dismissed the people in prayer.
Folks came up to me to thank me for the talk.
To offer their condolences, and tell me what a great
guy—what a great man—my dad was. Out of
respect for their memories, I just nodded and thanked
them for coming. And I waited until every last

person who wanted to speak to me, had a chance
to speak to me.

Finally I was alone with my dad. I was standing.
He was in his box. I walked over to him, and waited.
I placed my hand on his hands. Hands that worked
so hard. Held my mother in ecstatic embraces.
Hands that once held me. Hands that beat me.
His hands were no longer the full and thick hands of
a working man. They were cold, and thin. I waited
again. Waited to feel something. Maybe love.
Maybe grief. Maybe tears.

Nothing.

Except resentment.

"You son of a bitch, even now you are f'ing up
my life. You took away my vacation. Even from the
grave you are beating me. Even this…" My uncle
Onesimo walked into the chapel and interrupted my
thoughts. He had watery eyes.

"Poor guy," I thought. "He just lost his brother."

"I'm sorry, Tio," I said to him.

He hugged me, then he placed his hands on my dad's hands.

"Octavio, Octavio…" My uncle half-whispered as he started to weep.

"Poor guy," I thought again.

He stepped back and left the chapel.

Someone, somewhere, turned off the lights.

I closed his coffin and walked out.

Chapter Thirteen

SOMETHING WONDERFUL

Dave Bowman: You see, something's going to happen. You must leave.

Heywood Floyd: What? What's going to happen?

DB: Something wonderful.

HF: What?

DB: I understand how you feel. You see, it's all very clear to me now. The whole thing. It's wonderful.[15]

— *2001: A Space Odyssey*

However, as it is written:

"What no eye has seen, what no ear has heard,

and what no human mind has conceived"—

the things God has prepared for those who love him.[16]

— *Saint Paul*

When God chooses to speak to you, the whole universe is His voice. Movies, music, billboards, commercials… all become His platform.
It's as if there's a conspiracy to get your attention. Everything, and I mean everything, can be used by God to get your attention. In hindsight, I didn't realize I was being set up. I didn't know I was playing hide-and-go-seek with God. Through multiple sermons, movies, and conversations with people, I saw in the winter of 2005 that for years God had been trying to have a conversation with me that I refused to have with him.

I like Stanley Kubrick's film, *2001: A Space Odyssey*. I don't think I understand it. I don't know if anyone really does. But years later, when I saw the exchange between Dave Bowman and Heywood Floyd, I heard it differently. Truth? I love the the answer Dave Bowman gave to Heywood; I love those words: "Something wonderful."

I heard it like this:

Jesus: You see, something's going to happen. You must leave.

Me: What? What's going to happen?

Jesus: Something wonderful.

Me: What?

Jesus: I understand how you feel. You see, soon it'll be very clear to you. The whole thing. It's wonderful.

Before the end of of 2004 I would experience what I can only call a vision and a healing and a release.

It was unexpected.

It was emotional.

It was powerful.

And it was something wonderful.

Chapter Fourteen

WINTER OF 2004

Now Moses was tending the flock
of Jethro his father-in-law,
the priest of Midian, and he led
the flock to the far side of
the wilderness and came to Horeb,
the mountain of God.

There the angel of the Lord
appeared to him in flames of fire
from within a bush.

Moses saw that though the bush
was on fire it did not burn up.

So Moses thought, I will go over
and see this strange sight—
why the bush does not burn up.

When the Lord saw that he
had gone over to look, God called
to him from within the bush,
"Moses! Moses!"

And Moses said, "Here I am." [17]

—Exodus 3

I had a job that took me all throughout Southern California. I would drive anywhere from the Antelope Valley to Indio. The high desert and the low desert. Downtown Los Angeles. The San Fernando Valley. You name it, and I probably have been in one of the malls—in any city throughout Southern California.

One day I was driving northbound on the 5 freeway headed to the Lancaster area. I think the city was Acton, California. Now with all apologies to the good citizens of Acton, there's no reason for me to go there except for a job.

Driving along the 5 freeway, I had what I can only explain as a vision. I was completely aware that I was driving on the freeway. I was conscious of the fact that I was driving my car. But I saw something else as clearly as I saw the fact that I was driving.

Pause that for a moment.

Now the weird part: many years ago while skating I broke my left arm right above the elbow. It was

considered a serious injury because it damaged
the growth area at the end of the humerus bone.
It was set in a cast. And I lived with that cast
for several weeks. When the cast was removed, my
already skinny arm had atrophied and was
now even skinnier. My arm hurt and I could not
fully extend it.

Here's the vision.

I saw myself as a small boy holding my arm. I was
sitting on the floor in front of the TV. It looked
like a color-desaturated scene—dark and grainy.
This was a memory I had not thought about—ever.
But immediately I knew the context of the moment.
I must have made some noise or something
to bother my dad. And when I did, he threw his size
9, heavy, black Florsheim wingtip shoe at me.
And it hit me—right on the arm. It hurt, but what
hurt most was how little he cared about me.
Or I thought he didn't care.

Still, I have learned to ask questions whenever

something unusual happens and this was unusual.

This was an un-summoned memory.

Why am I thinking this? Why am I seeing this?

In that moment, the scene began to change. As if

a camera was panning to the right, I began

to see the living room of the house where I grew

up in Huntington Park. Then I saw my father sitting

in his chair—a black faux leather recliner.

Time compressed and I understood everything.

He didn't want to be a man who hurt his family.

He didn't want to be that guy.

In a nanosecond I understood all the conversations

with God I had dodged, all the sermons I had heard,

written, and preached. I knew this was the

moment the seed of bitterness was planted in me.

But most of all, I knew what a terrible son

I had been to my Fathers: the one on earth by not

forgiving him and the one in heaven for not

yielding to His gentle request to forgive as I had

been forgiven.

I looked at my father… he was young, strong, and handsome, and I said, out loud, "I forgive you. Please forgive me." I pulled over and wept. I was free for the first time in years. I felt lighter and cleaner. I wept not in sorrow, but in gratitude.

A few weeks later, my son David was graduating from college. I was smiling thinking about his accomplishment. As I was driving to another mall, I thought about how good life was. How fortunate I was to have sons, and a daughter, to see them grow up and do well. And then I had a thought I had never had before: "I'm going to call Popi and tell him the good news."

Then it hit me.

He was dead.

Gone.

He'd never come back to me. I pulled over and wept all over again. I wept in gratitude because I had been set free. So free.

It was the Winter of 2004.

Chapter Fifteen

I BLAME YOU

YOU KNOW NOTHING AT ALL! YOU DO NOT REALIZE THAT IT IS BETTER FOR YOU THAT ONE MAN DIE FOR THE PEOPLE THAN THAT THE WHOLE NATION PERISH.[18]

—Caiaphas

I've spent many years counseling people as a pastor, as a police chaplain, as a sales manager and as a friend. I've learned there are several kinds of people you cannot help, but the most difficult are the people who will not take responsibility for themselves.

You just can't help them.

As long as they cannot (read, will not) own the part they play in their misery, and take responsibility for their lives, you cannot help them. Period.

And for years I was one of those people. For years,

I blamed my dad (and mom) for everything that I didn't like or hated about myself. I practiced my own private form of what French literary theorist René Girard called "the scapegoat mechanism" in his book, *The Scapegoat*. Here's how it works: when tension arises in human communities, the problem is solved by choosing someone to blame for the tension, someone to isolate, and someone to ostracize. In its most extreme form, the "scapegoat" is sacrificed for the sake of the community. By this "mechanism" we (often, unconsciously) choose someone to blame for our problems and kill them. That was simplified, but do you see hints of this in your work?

In your home?

In your soul?

What's the result? Peace—or some form of peace. The problem has been solved. The one to blame has been removed or eliminated from the community. Think of human sacrifice and executions, and you'll see why this is often sanctioned by religion or by the state. It would be difficult to find many cultures that did not practice a form of scapegoating violence. You can find it in the Bible.

Long before philosopher René Girard, before author Kenneth Burke, before Dostoyevsky, even before Shakespeare, the Bible spoke about the scapegoat mechanism.[19] However, the Bible shows us the way out of this endless, effete cycle of sacrifice and violence. In the Holy Book, the scapegoat mechanism is disabused of its power, and in its place a fresh view of humanity is unveiled: a view based on love, truth, compassion, kindness, and (wait for it)… forgiveness. But the biggest surprise is this: God identifies with the victim; God becomes the scapegoat.

My temper and anger, my father's fault.

My lack of education, his fault.

My bad teeth, yes, that too, was his fault.

I cannot think of one thing I did not blame him for.

Popi, you piece-of-shit dad, for all my shortcomings,

for all my misery, for all the limitations I've known,

I blame you.

And while I'm at it, I blame my mother too.

Chapter Sixteen

I FINALLY UNDERSTOOD MY MOM

Forgiveness allows you to remember the event without reliving the pain.

— OCM

Father, forgive them, for they do not know what they are doing.[20]

— Jesus of Nazareth

Then the master called the servant in.

'You wicked servant,' he said, 'I canceled all that debt of yours because you begged me to.

Shouldn't you have had mercy on your fellow servant just as I had on you?'[21]

— Jesus of Nazareth

I have a horizontal scar on my forehead about one inch long. When I furrow my eyebrows, it's concealed in the natural folds of my forehead. It's about fifty-plus years old. And right now, I can still feel it with my fingers.

I think I was eight or nine when my mother threw a hammer at my face, causing that scar. I'm not certain she actually meant to hit me in the face, but hey, even a broken clock is right twice a day. She nailed me with that hammer (pun intended).

I cried when the hammer hit me. Not because it hurt. At least not my face. It hurt me to know she would hurt me. I held my hands to my face, and I recall stomping my feet in place. I cried and screamed in desperation and fear. Immediately, I think she knew she crossed a line.

She came to me, grabbed me, took me to the bathroom, washed the blood off my face, dried my face, and applied paper towels as a bandage and Scotch tape to cover the wound. Hey, she improvised.

Then my dad came home. When he saw what happened, he was pissed.

In hindsight, I can think of several reasons why. Maybe she was the brakes for him. And now she had acted out in violence. Maybe he thought at least one of them should be the good parent, and he knew it wasn't him. Maybe… what does it matter?

I went to school the next morning. Mr. Duckworth (How can you forget a name like that?) asked me what happened to my forehead. I told him, "My mother hit me in the face with a hammer."

Because it had bled through a little, he sent me to the school nurse to take a look. Maybe he was hoping she would know what to do in this situation. I remember she was beautiful. Blonde, blue eyes, dressed in white with that adorable paper hat nurses used to wear. She gently asked me what happened, and I repeated what I told Mr. Duckworth, "My mother hit me in the face with a hammer."

She didn't judge.

She just cared.

Gently and carefully she examined the bandaging and said, "I'll leave it alone for now." I thought then she meant the bandage. She probably did, but she might have also meant the whole incident. I went back to class.

Eventually, the bandage came off. The visible wound healed. But the invisible wound just festered. It would be years before the falling out between my mother and me was resolved.

My mother was a talented, driven woman, but she lacked education. She was the bastard child of my grandmother and a French Diplomat who was stationed in Mexico. She never knew her father. Never was acknowledged by him. She made a life for herself: married my dad, moved to America, had one daughter, lost two kids through miscarriage, had me, and had my brother too. But she was forever sensitive to slights, perceived or real.

I've mentioned how my father and I are alike in many ways. And this similarity to my father was a source of anger and violence between my mother and me. If my mom was angry with me, my father caught it when he came home. If my mom was angry with my father, I knew I'd better walk on egg shells around her.

Once she screamed into my face, "I wish you had not been born!" I was six. I recall the time when in anger, she lifted me by the ears and moved me into another room where additional verbal abuse was hurled at me. I was seven. And when she and my dad were experiencing severe marital troubles, she hissed at me, "Your dad and I will probably divorce, and it's your fault." I was thirteen.

We continued to have a deteriorating relationship through my teenage years, then young adulthood. There were years we were not on speaking terms. I refused to let her see my kids—her grandkids. I also placed her, like my father, in a dark place called contempt.

At my 30th high school reunion, I sat at a table watching guests enter the banquet hall.

In walked this man I knew from high school. The funny thing is, I didn't like him in high school, and I immediately didn't like him at that reunion. Did I mention I was a pastor at the time? It's funny how you can excuse yourself of all the different shortcomings that you encourage others to process and deal with.

But I digress. So there was an empty seat next to me, and where did this person sit? You guessed it: right next to me. I did everything possible to signal I was not interested in talking to him. Eventually he initiated a conversation. I discovered he was also a follower of Jesus and attended the church I heard my mother had started attending.

When I found out my mother was attending church (some twenty-plus years earlier), she was in her early 50s. Cynically I said to myself, "That's just an old lady trying to get into heaven."

I asked this man if he knew my mother: "Do you know a woman named Carmen Martinez?"

He struggled to recall who that was. I described her as an older woman in her 70s, who waddled back and forth because of a bad hip. "Oh," he said, "Do you mean Sister Carmen?" I thought to myself, "Sister Carmen?! Good Lord, she has them fooled."

Then immediately he snapped his fingers and said, "You're Tavito." Now this is my childhood name that very few people know.

"She's always praying for you. She's always asking God to help you forgive her for all the hurt she caused you. And she prays for your church, too."

I'm not sure what you think or feel when you read this. I just knew that for many years, I was dodging responsibility to forgive so many people, including my father. My mother was another one.

I physically reacted to that information. My mother was an older woman, regretting some of the things she did, and I was a pastor who often proclaimed God's forgiveness, but refused to give it to her. Here's my mother, asking the good Lord to help me forgive her. I left the party early, drove to the airport for a red-eye to Boston that night to speak to a group of pastors about… Wait for it… forgiveness.

When I returned, I made the effort to connect with my mother and restore that relationship. It was health-giving, and it was a good step in the direction of total freedom and healing.

Years later, my mother had a hip replacement she needed. I went to go visit her at the hospital where she was recovering. She was lucid and awake, and we talked for almost an hour. As I was about to leave, she grabbed me by the wrist and said, "Tavo, have you ever forgiven me for all the things I did to you?" I replied, "Mom, of course I did. Please. I'm so sorry you think I haven't. We're good."

She said, "I just need to hear you say it. I just need to hear you say, 'I forgive you.'"

I held her hand and I looked her in the eye while we both wept. "Mom, I forgive you. Please accept my forgiveness; it's total and complete. I hold nothing against you."

Then I said, "Would you do me a favor? Would you pray for me?"

"Yes," was her reply.

And I knelt on the floor next to her bed. She placed her hand on top of my head and began to pray. She thanked God for His kindness, for His power to heal and restore, His mercy in resurrecting what was once dead.

Entering those moments, I was filled with gratitude because this was the woman who gave me physical life. And now we were both before God as brother and sister. Often I'm still amazed at his kindness towards both of us.

Two weeks before she died, we spoke for thirty minutes over the phone. She called to tell me she was dying of cancer. There was no fear in her voice, no anger or bitterness. "I'm tired and ready to go home," she told me. For two seconds, there was silence. Then I thanked her for all the things she did for me: the time she stayed up all night nursing my swollen broken arm, for teaching me basic cooking skills, and how to iron, sew, and clean. I thanked her for taking me to museums, dance classes, and piano lessons.

I thanked her for sending me to catechism and taking me to church. I reminded her of all the things she did that I was grateful for. I told her she was a good mom, and I told her I loved her.

I told her all the things she did for me that mattered.

But most of all, I thanked her for sending me and my brother and sister to Saturday catechism, for taking the family to mass on Sundays, where I learned there was a God and I was not him. Nor was I the center of the universe.

Carmen Maria Martinez died the day after Thanksgiving in 2014.

Years later, I hurt and let down someone who was very close to me. We worked through it. But it was hard. She and her husband forgave me, and I was grateful. There was no reluctance in our interactions. There was no sense they were holding back in the friendship.

Yet one day after service, I walked over to them both. I mumbled something that I do not recall. But I did manage to ask, "Do you forgive me?" They answered, "Of course we do." I told them I believed them. They had proven it over and over, but I needed to know. I needed to hear it. "Would you please tell me? I just need to hear it." Graciously, they obliged me. At that moment, I understood my mom.

Chapter Seventeen

WHAT FORGIVENESS ISN'T

THE WEAK CAN NEVER FORGIVE. FORGIVENESS IS THE ATTRIBUTE OF THE STRONG.[22]   —*Mahatma Gandhi*

Forgiveness is not JUSTICE.

Between resentment and revenge is fairness; forgiveness is not on the continuum. There is nothing just about forgiveness. When you are cleared of a debt, you are "forgiven" the debt. It is called forgiveness instead of "paid in full," because—well, there was no payment. Forgiveness is not a "payment." Forgiveness is not a transaction.
In relationships, actual forgiveness can restore the forgiver and the forgiven; it can restore friendly relations between the two. Forgiveness may do more, but at the very least, it can begin to accomplish the restoration of a relationship.

Another word for justice is fairness; forgiveness is not fair either. Forgiveness only needs two people:

one who needs forgiveness and one who needs to forgive. Forgiveness does not require a balanced scale of justice. We may want restitution for what has happened before we will forgive. This shows we value fairness or justice over relationship or forgiveness. And if this is true of you, that's okay, but that's not forgiveness.

And forgiveness does not require an apology from the offender; sometimes, they are dead or absent, or they refuse to admit fault. With forgiveness, there's no need for an explanation from you to them explaining how they've hurt you.

If you say or think, "When _____ happens, then I will (or can) forgive," well, then you are not forgiving at all. You're only setting the price to buy "forgiveness" from you. Forgiveness is not a transaction in that way. Forgiveness is not justice; it's a choice.

Forgiveness is not DISTANCE.

Forgiveness is not distance. Some of us have dealt

with the person who hurt us by moving emotionally or physically away from them. We moved as far as we could to avoid being hurt again, or being reminded of the hurt they caused us. Some of us moved to "keep the peace." We moved to avoid any potential confrontation. We also moved away thinking (hoping) that the distance (and time) would help us. It won't. The myth of "moving away from toxic people" is one of the the worst deceptions—one that prevents us from ever resolving the wounds we have.

In September 2014, I moved into a new old home. An amazing side-gabled Craftsman-style home built in 1910. Within two weeks, I made three hospital visits as the result of four injuries: I fell off a six-foot ladder with light bulbs in my hands, which resulted in bits of broken glass embedded in my palms; I slashed the top of my left hand with a razor; I shattered my right index finger; and I broke the outer metatarsal bone of my left foot. Now what I didn't do was move out of my home.

I went to a doctor for stitches, x-rays, antibiotics, and a bottle of 800mg ibuprofen.

Forgiveness works like that. You can move away, but you're still cut, shattered, or broken. Or all three. With this (emotional, mental, spiritual) injury, you need healing, not distance, because distance doesn't cure anything.

Forgiveness is not distance; it's healing.

Forgiveness is not TRUST.

Everyone has been disappointed by someone else. Some of us have been taken advantage of, stolen from, molested, lied to, cheated on… or just generally let down by people who should have done better. A lot better. Forgiveness will heal you, release you from pain and even give you new eyes to reinterpret the past (more on that later), but it won't automatically make the offender a better person. Forgiveness is freedom for you, but does not require a restoration of trust. Forgiveness is about the past; trust is about the future.

Forgiveness is given. Trust must be earned.

Forgiveness is not trust; it's freedom.

Forgiveness is a choice, it's healing, and it's freedom.

If you don't forgive, then you're drinking poison and hoping the other person will die.

Sometimes, we need to forgive.

Sometimes, we need to be forgiven.

Sometimes, the only fix is forgiveness.

Chapter Eighteen

THE BRONZE SNAKE AND THE LAWN SPRINKLER

So Moses made a bronze snake and put it up on a pole. Then when anyone was bitten by a snake and looked at the bronze snake, they lived.[23]

— *Book of Numbers*

Just as Moses lifted up the snake in the wilderness, so the Son of Man must be lifted up.[24]

— *Jesus of Nazareth*

It would be funny if it weren't so pathetic.

And sad.

When I knew I had done "something wrong," before my mom spanked me, before my dad would beat me, before any punishment: I took care of it myself. Here's what I would do:

I would slip outside the house. I would walk to the patio where our lemon tree was, then over to the door that opened into the garage. I'd go in and close the door behind me. I'd walk over to the table where the gardening tools were. I'd sift through some of it, and when I found what I was looking for, I'd pull it out and off the table.

A brass sprinkler head.

Metal and materials have meanings in the Scriptures. Silver is the metal of redemption. Brass, the metal of judgment. Moses learned that. Jesus knew that. I had no idea of that when I went into the garage to punish myself.

So I'd take that sprinkler head and smash it down
on my hand. My left hand. Then I'd hit my face.
Then my hand again. I'd stop when the pain
was greater than the fear of hurting myself. This
wasn't the last time I hurt myself.

Or my hands.

Years later, I punished myself again. That time
I scarred up my right hand pretty good and broke
three bones in my left hand. The girlfriend
I had at the time drove me to the hospital. My pants
were bloody; I was in pain and embarrassed.

Because of debris in the wounds, the hospital staff
soaked my hands in bowls of iodine. For some
reason, not as painful as you'd think it would be.
The nurse and doctors picked out the bits
of dirt and debris in those wounds. I winced and
jerked in pain. One of the doctors said that was a
good sign. The nerves were still intact.

I asked the doctor if I would ever be able to play the
piano after this. He looked me in the eyes,

and in a soft voice, he said, "I'm going to do everything possible for you to recapture all of your original motion. I promise you." I looked back at him and replied, "That's great, because I could never play the piano before." It took him a moment to get it. He quietly laughed. Then he told me, "You just got out of a 72-hour hold." (What's a 72-hour hold? It's part of the Welfare and Institutions Code, which allows a person who is a danger to themselves to be involuntarily detained for a 72-hour psychiatric hospitalization. So there's that.)

Because of the swelling, they could not put my left hand in a cast. So they set the bones as best they could and secured my left hand in a splint. My right hand they cleaned and bandaged. I had to come back the next day for an examination by an orthopedic specialist.

For years I didn't tell anyone this story. I was too embarrassed. But for several years after this incident, whenever it was cold, the scars on my hands

would turn blue and purple. Eventually somebody
would always notice. I've made up stories
about the fight, or an accident, or just ignored the
question to make some dumb joke. But the
truth is: I self-injured. I had scars, but they were
only visible scars.

The invisible acts of self-injury never scar up
and never heal on their own. In my unwillingness to
forgive, I was bleeding out of my soul. I never
had forgiven my father, or people at school and
work, or anybody who had ever harmed me.
Real and imagined. And for the times that I couldn't
"make things right" by an act of violence like
stabbing, fistfights, or verbal abuse, I continued to
be filled with anger and hatred. I carried all
that crap inside me.

Years later, and I mean years, those scars on my
hands finally healed. Cold days did not cause a
change in color. Unless you knew they were
there, you wouldn't notice them. Then something
changed. No longer a reminder of my shame,

those scars became a reminder of God's kindness and forgiveness to me. And several years after that,
I decided to cover my hands in tattoos that pointed to my gratitude for this: I have been forgiven,
and I had learned to forgive others. I wanted my hands: hands which once pointed to my
darkness, my self-destruction, my anger, and my hatred, now to point others to love.

My first tattoos are on my hands.

All of them have a spiritual meaning.

All of them point to my restoration.

Love covers.

LOVE WINS.

Chapter Nineteen

I FEASTED AND FORCED OTHERS TO STARVE

Simon, I have something to tell you.[25] — *Jesus of Nazareth*

Whether you do or do not take the stories of Jesus seriously, there is wisdom in His lifestyle and words for living. This story about Jesus eating at the home of a religious leader is a good one. It starts with a dinner invitation and ends with a divine invitation. It's found in Dr. Luke's biography of Jesus, chapter seven. It goes like this:

One of the Pharisees asked him over for a meal. He went to the Pharisee's house and sat down at the dinner table. Just then a woman of the village, the town harlot, having learned that Jesus was a guest in the home of the Pharisee, came with a bottle of very expensive perfume and stood at his feet, weeping, raining tears on his feet. Letting down her hair, she dried his feet, kissed them, and anointed them with the perfume. When the Pharisee who had invited him saw this, he said to himself, "If this man was the prophet I thought he was, he would have known what kind of woman this is who is falling all over him."

Jesus said to him, "Simon, I have something to tell you."

"Oh? Tell me."

"Two men were in debt to a banker. One owed five hundred silver pieces, the other fifty. Neither of them could pay up, and so the banker canceled both debts. Which of the two would be more grateful?"

Simon answered, "I suppose the one who was forgiven the most."

"That's right," said Jesus. Then turning to the woman, but speaking to Simon, he said, "Do you see this woman? I came to your home; you provided no water for my feet, but she rained tears on my feet and dried them with her hair. You gave me no greeting, but from the time I arrived she hasn't quit kissing my feet. You provided

nothing for freshening up, but she has soothed
my feet with perfume. Impressive, isn't it?
She was forgiven many, many sins, and so she is very,
very grateful. If the forgiveness is minimal,
the gratitude is minimal."

Then he spoke to her: "I forgive your sins."

That set the dinner guests talking behind his back,
"Who does he think he is, forgiving sins!"
He ignored them and said to the woman, "Your faith
has saved you. Go in peace."

Here are some observations: When Simon asked
Jesus over for dinner, Simon was inviting Jesus
into an intimate situation. And as a Pharisee, Simon
had a tremendous amount of influence in the
culture of Jesus' time. Jesus, not so much. Not yet at
least. Then as now, in Middle Eastern culture,
eating together was an act of intimacy. At a real level,
you were binding yourself to the person you
ate with. In the act of eating together, you said,
"The food which nourishes my body nourishes your

body too."

So something about the life of Jesus was important, or at least interesting to Simon.

Next, there's this woman. So the men are eating. Members of a strict religious order, and Jesus. A local whore finds out about this luncheon, goes there and lets herself in. She brings a gift, too—a jar of perfume. She washes the feet of Jesus with her tears, dries them with her hair, lotions them with the perfume. Now, if this seems weird, or awkward… wait for it.

In the West, we all agree on what is the dirtiest part of our body: below the waist, and above the knees. You know. Don't make me say it. But in this culture and time, it was the feet. Even today, in Middle Eastern culture, it is rude to show the bottoms of your feet.

And yet, maybe this woman was experiencing what years earlier a spokesperson for the God of her race and country said, "How beautiful on the mountains

are the feet of those who bring good news,
who proclaim peace, who bring good tidings, who
proclaim salvation, who say to Zion, 'Your God
reigns!'" —The Hebrew prophet Isaiah

This sentiment would be echoed later by Saint Paul
in his letter to the Roman followers of Jesus,
"And how can anyone preach unless they are sent?
As it is written, 'How beautiful are the feet of
those who bring good news!'"

And wiping a man's feet with her hair? Well, at that
time, a woman's hair was a significant part of
her beauty. Her glory. And the lotion? Expensive.
It probably helped her make a living selling sex.
So picture this, the woman is crying over the feet of
Jesus and then drying them with her hair.
Simon sees this. Everyone did, but only his thoughts
are recorded for us: "If this man was the prophet
I thought he was, he would have known what kind
of woman this is who is falling all over him."

What else can you see? A person who cleans the

lowest part of Jesus' body, with the best she had to offer, maybe the only thing she could offer— her hair and her perfume. They were an important part of her beauty and an important part of her income. They're nothing to her now.

Why?

Forgiveness.

She's free.

A few years later, Saint Paul would write something similar: "Yes, all the things I once thought were so important are gone from my life. Compared to the high privilege of knowing Christ Jesus as my Master, firsthand, everything I once thought I had going for me is insignificant—dog dung…"

Yep.

Poop.

Canine poop specifically.

Thank you, Saint Paul, for that visual.

Jesus was dialed into God in a way none of us are. Some saints and mystics come close, but clearly they are not Jesus; He was a prophet and He knew who this woman was. And He was going to tell Simon, so he would know.

For many years I have thought about forgiveness, studied forgiveness, and tried to live out forgiveness in my life. Sometimes it went better than others. Sometimes I completely fell short of the ideal. I've questioned and wondered about forgiveness: is it a mental, or emotional, or therapeutic exercise? Is it a spiritual, mystical event? Is it my duty as a follower of Jesus? Do I need to believe in God, or a god, or a higher power to forgive?

What I do know is this: when you choose not to forgive somebody, especially if you are a follower of Jesus, it's like feasting at the banquet table of forgiveness from God and refusing someone else a crumb. And that is exactly what I did, for years.

I feasted, and forced others to starve.

Chapter Twenty

HONOR YOUR MOTHER AND FATHER - I

HONOR YOUR...MOTHER SO THAT YOU'LL LIVE A LONG TIME IN THE LAND THAT GOD, YOUR GOD, IS GIVING YOU.[26]

— Exodus 20

THE HEART OF A MOTHER IS A DEEP ABYSS AT THE BOTTOM OF WHICH YOU WILL ALWAYS FIND FORGIVENESS.

— Honoré de Balzac

My mother was a beautiful woman.

From the photos I've seen of her and memories I have of her, she always looked "put together." She grew up in the era when women did their hair and makeup every day, and she was no different. She curled her hair with pink foam curlers, wore lipstick, painted her nails, and always smelled

of perfume. Every day. Most nights, she would
slather a layer of POND'S cold cream on her face.

In her purse, she carried a compact. The way women
used to do. The compact had a small mirror,
and a powder cake she used to lightly pat away the
shine on her nose and forehead. In the mornings,
I used to watch her when she applied her
makeup and styled her hair. I wanted to be a hair
stylist and makeup artist because of those moments.
She was curvy, about 5'5", and 140 pounds of
pure femininity: elegant and strong. Because of her,
I love the smell of perfume and smoke
on a woman. Especially if she is "put together."
Hey— don't judge what you don't understand.

She loved God and the Catholic Church. But she
also took birth control. So once a year
she would keep her standing appointment with
Monsignor Shear to plead her case as to
why she should be allowed to take communion.
And once a year, the monsignor would relent
and grant her the most important of the seven

sacraments of the Church. I admire her for that.

She was also clean and organized. I mean c-l-e-a-n.
Dusting and mopping floors, folding and arranging
clothes, maintaining the front and back yards,
and making sure her kids toed the line as well.
Did I mention she would iron bed linens?
Good Lord, I love that still. In my mind, Saturdays
are for cleaning, ironing, and deep grooming—
everywhere (I'll stop right here).

And the best Saturday nights, the best sleep is after a
day of cleaning, grooming and then lying in
a bed with freshly washed (and bonus points, ironed)
linens. Most nights I like to spritz a bit of scent
before I go to bed, too. It's the best. All because of
my mom—or "Mommy," as I always called her.
Until the day she died, I could never call her
anything else.

For many years, we did not have a good relationship.
That's on me. I knew better. Well, I should have
known better. I was exposed to the teachings of Jesus

on forgiveness and understood the mental,
emotional, and spiritual benefits of forgiveness.
It's amazing the blind spots we can have.
There were slights and insults we hurled at
each other.

Goodness, I have no idea how that must have
hurt my Mommy. To have her son scream hate-filled
screeds in her direction. She was not capable of
helping me or herself. She was too proud and so was I.

Our reconciliation began at Christmas in 1989.

I was visiting my sister Dora in her home to
exchange gifts. It had been five years since my mother
had seen my kids. Why? Punishment. She insulted
my wife. I banished her until she apologized.
My idea. I know, I was a real douchebag. Yet every
year, my mother would buy and make gifts
for my kids. She would send them through my sister.
One of the most special gifts was knitted house
slippers, which fit like a sock over a foot—literally.
She would knit a pair for each of my kids every year.

My mom called Dora so she could pick up the
gifts she had for my kids. She had no idea I was at
Dora's home. My sister was about to leave when
she suggested it was time. Time to let go of whatever
the hell I was doing and allow her to take
my kids to see their paternal grandmother. It was
Christmas. I had the time, so I relented, but
I did not go with them. I can imagine what a treat
that must have been for my mother and my kids.

That moment was the beginning of softening my
heart towards my mother. Providence was
working in my favor even when I was against any
attempt at reconciliation. Because not long
after that night, I attended my 30th high school
reunion—the night I heard how my mother
was always praying for me.

Right now, I wish to share how great my
Mommy was.

I recall how she stayed by my side all night when
I broke my arm. It had to remain elevated and iced.

So while I slept, she would continually change
the ice pack, and adjust the pillows which held my
arm up above my chest.

All night.

When I was small, after each bath, she would dry me
off, rub Jergens lotion on my arms and legs
(no ashy kids here) and throw on a little scent, too.
Agua Lavanda Puig eau de cologne was a favorite.
She taught me how to comb my hair, wash my face,
clean my ears, wash and fold clothes, iron, clean
and organize my belongings.

And she took me to museums. She would stand me
in front of art pieces and ask, "Tavo, what do you
see?" I specifically remember the first time we
went to the the Huntington Library in San Marino,
CA. I was enthralled by the idea that the impressive
museum was once someone's home. I saw a
Gutenberg Bible there. Okay, I touched it, too.

But what stopped me in my tracks was the painting
by Thomas Gainsborough called "The Blue Boy,"

a full-length portrait in oil. Why? Because in our modest middle-class home in Huntington Park, my mom hung a copy of that painting in the dining room. I had looked at that print many times, but when I saw it in person, I fell in love with art—portraits, to be exact. My Mom was my first art teacher. I have shared this story and the experience with only one other person. It is that special to me.

The Notebook

On the morning after mom died, my brother Cesar called. He had just heard from our sister Dora. I drove over to the bungalow my mother had lived in on Mission Place in Huntington Park. Dora greeted me at the door. We both wept for a few moments and then I went into the bedroom where she had slept, and now rested. I came out, sat in the living room, and Dora joined me. Cesar arrived a bit later. While we sat, Dora asked me if Mom had already told me about "my notebook."

"What are you talking about?" I asked.

She replied, "Oh, wait."

Dora disappeared down the hall and returned with a three-inch, three-ring, navy blue notebook. She handed it to me. Inside, arranged in chronological order, were photos—of me—of my parents—of my sister and brother—of my first family. These were all the years I thought I had lost. There were also my report cards, newspaper clippings about me, the card from the bouquet of flowers my dad gave her at the occasion of my birth, and religious cards I had inscribed. A letter I had written to my mom dated 1984.

But there was more to come.

My mom kept anything and everything that involved me. And my Mom gave instructions to Dora to give me the Bible I had given to mom over forty years earlier. It was worn out, underlined, annotated, and obviously often-read.

As I flipped through the history of my life, Dora interrupted my thoughts, "Mom also said she wanted you to officiate her funeral."

"When did she say this? Of course I will."

"She also said you would know the verse she wanted read at her service."

"Dora, I have no idea what Mom wanted read."

"Some verse from the Bible about running."

I knew immediately: *"I have fought the good fight, I have finished the race, I have kept the faith. Now there is in store for me the crown of righteousness, which the Lord, the righteous Judge, will award to me on that day—and not only to me, but also to all who have longed for his appearing."* These are some of the last words Saint Paul wrote to a young man, a pastor named Timothy.

I officiated my mother's funeral on November 29th, 2014.

She is buried at Rose Hills, in Whittier, CA.

And at her service, I read that verse.

In her honor.

Mommy,

I love and miss you.

Your Son,

Tavito

Chapter Twenty-One

HONOR YOUR MOTHER AND FATHER - I I

HONOR YOUR FATHER...
SO THAT YOU'LL LIVE A LONG
TIME IN THE LAND THAT GOD,
YOUR GOD, IS GIVING YOU.[27]

— *Exodus 20*

LUX AETERNA, LIBERA ME

— *Gabriel Fauré, Requiem in D Minor, Op. 48*

OUR LACK OF FREEDOM LIES
RIGHT IN THE MIDDLE OF OUR
NEED AND OUR WILLINGNESS
TO FORGIVE.

SOMETIMES WE HAVE NO
PERCEIVED NEED TO FORGIVE.

SOMETIMES WE HAVE NO
WILLINGNESS TO FORGIVE.

AND SOMETIMES, WE PREFER
TO STAY SICK.

— *OCM*

Ever stop to think about the Ten Commandments?
Probably not.

Here's a thought: like wine, they're not for children.

Many well-meaning but misguided Sunday School
teachers and parents teach the fifth commandment
as if it was written to kids. And that's too bad,
because all of the commandments were intended for
adults, not children.

Until fourteen years ago, the fifth commandment
made no sense to me. How does one honor
a father who was so contemptible? Here's how:
forgiveness. Forgiveness is the freedom from your
past that allows you to re-interpret your past.
Oh, you can recall what really sucked, but it no
longer has a hold on you.

Daddy issues are cliché until they aren't.
From over-sexualized, slutty women, to out of
control, violent men, adults with daddy issues
are colored, textured, and twisted into sub-humans.
I know I was. Maybe you were (or are) too.

So, in no particular order, this is my feeble attempt to honor the man whose name I bear and whom I resemble in many, many ways.

- My love of clothes, colognes, and being well-groomed— from my father.

- My name, my appearance, my nose, my ears, almost every physical attribute — from my father.

- My love of food, because of my father.

- My love of music — comes from him.

- Think I'm funny? My father was funnier. All the time.

- I make friends easily, but my father was a master of making friends.

- He taught me to never poke fun at anyone less fortunate than me. Never.

- He danced (I never learned).

- He took me to swimming lessons (I never learned that, either) and to beaches and campsites (I never learned to enjoy those as well).

- He taught me how to paint homes, fix things around the house, use tools, and take care of cars (I learned, but I won't do it).

- He bought me a brand new car for my high school graduation (yes, high school).

- He took me to musicals and to the symphony.

- I saw him embrace my mom. Often.

- I learned my view of marriage from him.

- What I know about physical affection, I learned from my father.

- He was generous to a fault (check).

- He was careless with money (ditto) and, overall, a decent guy.

After I forgave my parents, more and more memories came back. Not negative ones, healthy and kind ones. Here are two about my father:

I had done something wrong—I don't recall now what it was, but my dad was supposed to "spank" me before he left for work. Unfortunately for me, my friend John Swanson came over to play. I was cringing with dread as John and I played together. My father, now showered and dressed for work, came out and called me over to him. I walked the Green Mile to him, expecting to be slapped, hit, yelled at—or all three. Instead, he said: "You know you're supposed to be spanked, but your friend is here and I don't want to embarrass you. Don't do (whatever I did) again." Then he kissed me goodbye as he left for work. I don't recall what I did after that, but I do recall what I felt: loyalty to him and love for him. He showed mercy and respected me as a person.

The second restored memory is this:

On the night I injured myself, breaking my hands, a girlfriend drove me home because I could not grip the steering wheel or stick shift of my 1970 240Z 4-speed. My mother was waiting for me at the doorway of our home and only winced when she saw my bandaged hands and bloody jeans. And she was smoking again— a habit she had given up years earlier. I walked past her into the living room, and sat on the sofa. I sat there—ashamed and defeated. And I waited; it didn't take long.

My mother lit into me.

She yelled at me about how what I did affected her—how I was selfish and foolish—how I failed her and how this event "was just like you." In my defense, to stop my mother, I resorted to the only thing I had left: my voice. "Leave me the hell alone!" I yelled as I kicked the coffee table away. The truth is, I didn't want to be left alone. I wanted her to hold me, and tell me it was going to be okay, but it wasn't only my hands that were broken, I was broken.

And so was my mom.

Then the worst thing happened. My father came
out of the bedroom. He was angry and
probably tired from working all night. He went to
my mom, gathered her up and said to her,
"Leave him alone. If he wants to be this, let him."
They walked back into their room and I got
my wish. I was left alone. I sat there for ten minutes
or so, weeping in humiliation.

Then the best thing happened. After a few minutes,
my dad came back into the living room.
He had tears running down his face. He walked
over to me. He helped me up, guided me
to my bedroom, and sat me on my bed. And then,
he got down on his knees and removed my shoes.
Gently, he helped me out of my jacket and
carefully assisted me to get under the covers, and
into bed. All the while, he wept. When I was
in bed, he leaned over and kissed me goodnight.
Then he left the room. He didn't say a word.

The next morning, he entered my room, dressed
as always. He got me dressed and drove me
to the hospital to get my bandages changed.
And for some reason, he said, "I'm sorry, Tavo."
After we arrived home, he kissed my mom and me
goodbye and left for work.

But possibly the most powerful, indelible, restored
memory I have of my father is this: Every
night when he came home, I would hear him open
the garage door. He'd drive his GM Pontiac
into the garage and park it. It would rumble into
silence as if it knew it was time to rest. Then my
father would close the garage door and walk
three steps to our front door. Inserting his key to
turn the door lock, the front door would
reluctantly creak open. He'd tiptoe in, but we had
wood floors, so it wasn't very effective.

And every night when he came home — and I mean
every night — he'd walk past his bedroom where
he and my mom slept and into the bedroom I shared
with my brother.

Then it would happen. I slept on the top bunk, so I went first.

He would kiss me.

On the cheek.

Every night.

I was first.

And sometimes, if the room was cold, he'd slip off his coat and cover me.

Then he'd kiss my brother.

Adjust his blankets, too.

Then he'd kiss my sister in her room.

Then he'd go to his room.

To this day, I still kiss my family and friends on the cheek.

Just like my father did.

And when I do, I'm saying, I love you.

Just like my father did.

There are days I miss my father so much, that I weep over his absence.

I would have loved for him to see his successful and handsome grandsons.

He would have loved their wives, too.

And they would have loved him.

I wish he could have seen his beautiful and talented granddaughter.

She would have taken the time to explain the art, music, and fashion she writes about.

And she shares his love of French culture.

But most of all,

I just miss my father.

I would love to have him around.

And if he napped like old men do,

I would tiptoe into his room,

Kiss him on his cheek,

And,

if the room was cold,

I would slip off my coat to cover him.

Popi,

I love you and miss you.

Your son,

Tavito

Chapter Twenty-Two

HOW OR WHY SHOULD I FORGIVE OTHERS?

Resentment is like drinking poison and then hoping it will kill your enemies.[28]

—Nelson Mandela

Forgiveness doesn't require a specific—or even any—religious tradition. It only requires you to rid yourself of emotional baggage through forgiveness. Why? Because then you become free. And that freedom manifests differently in people. It could be: an increased effectiveness in your leadership, your creative output shoots up unexpectedly, your physical stamina soars, or your ability to enjoy life and relationships expands.

All because you practice forgiveness. From forgiving the guy who cut you off on the freeway to the grand betrayal in your life. All of us need to forgive someone. Remember, forgiveness is not about the other person, it's about you. Of course forgiveness may free the one who harmed you—even if they're dead, in denial, or remorseless—but you're free. The person forgiveness frees, is you. And that's when the benefits of freedom kick in.

Forgiveness frees you from past hurts, pain and betrayals. You become free of your need for an apology or for justice before you experience peace. Your ability to love people returns. Now this does not mean what happened was okay, or that you allow that person to hurt you again. It does mean you are free.

And there's still more. Forgiving others helps you accept forgiveness. Forgiven people become forgiving people.

So how does one forgive?

There are three types of forgiveness and each one applies in different situations. Knowing this, it'll be easier to understand what forgiveness is—I've already shared what it is not. (I owe a debt to UCLA psychiatrist Dr. Stephen Marmer for his explanation of forgiveness.) [29]

Forgive and Forget

Most people understand forgiveness in terms of forgive and forget. But this type of forgiveness does not apply to all situations which require us to forgive. It is specific to unique circumstances. When should you forgive and forget? When a child breaks something, when someone truly did not understand what they did wrong, if the person is incapable of taking responsibility for their actions due to a lack of maturity or skills...

And finally: when someone sincerely apologizes for the harm they caused and there is a reasonable expectation the event will not happen again, then the healthy response is to forgive that person and to completely, without reservation, absolve them.

Forgive and Watch

This one is more difficult and requires more patience on our part. When someone offers a partial apology, or an insincere apology, or apologizes but

blames you for their bad behavior, then you need
to forgive and watch. This person has not
(and may never) fully accepted the responsibility
of their actions. However, you still need to forgive,
for your own mental and emotional well-being.

Do you trust them again?

Do you restore the relationship?

Maybe.

You'll need to watch to see if that person can be
trusted again. In time, forgive and watch can become
forgive and forget, but only after time has passed.

Forgive and Be Free

The third and final type of forgiveness is this: forgive
and be free. This is almost identical to forgive
and forget, but no apology is involved. Maybe the
person cannot, or will not apologize. Maybe they're
dead, gone, unreachable, or they simply refuse
to apologize. No matter.

Remember, first of all, forgiveness is more for you—
to be free—to be healthy—than it is for the
other person. Their apology isn't necessary.
With forgive and be free, you are released of the
millstone of bitterness, the poison of resentment.
You are free of carrying the hurt with you,
and spreading it to others.

Those are the three types of forgiveness.

Forgiveness is a means of grace and health for
both parties.

Why should you forgive?

Because it is insanity to carry the poison of unforgiveness.

Chapter Twenty-Three

EPILOGUE

My journey ends right about here.
Yours may just be starting.

–OCM

I wrote this to tell you of your need to forgive.

In the West, we love the idea of forgiveness.

We see the need to forgive and to be forgiven.

To say you must forgive is easy—cheap, even.
But I've learned to forgive.

So can you.

I've shared why you should forgive, how to forgive,
and now you decide what to do.

The things that happened to me as a small boy,
I would not wish on anyone.

Yet I'm glad those things happened to me.

I love the things I wish had not happened.

All of them.

After all, how can you help the wounded unless
you have wounds of your own?

I've learned about forgiveness and I learned
to forgive.

This is what I know:

Forgiveness is freedom.

Forgiveness is life.

Do you want to be forgiven?

Do you want to live?

Then forgive.

*This is why I can say: it was a beautiful day
when my father died.*

Endnotes

1. *2 Corinthians 1:3-5 (New International Version (NIV))*
2. *Fielding, Thomas, editor. Select Proverbs of All Nations. London, D. S. Maurice, Fenchurch Street, 1824, p. 216.*
3. *Asinaria . Written by Titus Plautus 495.*
4. *Matthew 18:28-30 (NIV)*
5. *Ephesians 4:31-32 (NIV)*
6. *Exodus 20:5 (NIV)*
7. *Exodus 20:6 (NIV)*
8. *Mamet, David, writer. The Untouchables. Performance by Kevin Costner, Paramount Pictures, 1987.*
9. *Romans 7:21-23 (NIV)*
10. *Luke 12:22-24 (THE MESSAGE (MSG))*
11. *Mark 11:25 (NIV)*
12. *Ephesians 4:31-32 (MSG)*
13. *Matthew 18:21-22 (NIV)*
14. *The Gift Poems by Hafez The Great Sufi Master. Translated by Daniel Ladner, New York, Penguin Compass, 1999, p. 23.*
15. *Kubrick, Stanley, writer. 2001: A Space Odyssey. Performances by Keir Dullea and William Sylvester, Metro-GoldwynMayer, 1968.*
16. *1 Corinthians 2:9 (NIV)*
17. *Exodus 3:1-4 (NIV)*
18. *John 11:49-50 (NIV)*
19. *Scapegoat reference is found in Leviticus 16:20-22*
20. *Luke 23:34 (NIV)*
21. *Matthew 18:32-33 (NIV)*
22. *This famous quote is generally attributed to Gandhi*
23. *Numbers 21:9 (NIV)*
24. *John 3:14 (NIV)*
25. *Luke 7:40 (NIV)*
26. *Exodus 20:12 (MSG)*

27. *Ibid*
28. *This famous quote is generally attributed to Nelson Mandela*
29. *For a complete review of Marmer's work on forgiveness, please refer to: Marmer, Dr. Stephen. https://www.prageru.com, 5 May 2014, www.prageru.com/videos/forgiveness.*

OCM refers to the author, Octavio Cesar Martinez

Commendations

I AM GRATEFUL TO CALL THESE TERRIFIC HUMAN BEINGS MY FRIENDS; ALL OF THEM ARE CREATIVE, SELFLESS LEADERS AND SERVANTS. THANK YOU FOR YOUR ENDORSEMENT OF MY BOOK.

An authentic accounting and reflection on the ambivalent relationship between a son and father in a time when the world is crying out for authenticity. This work will beg you to read on and understand how the author resolved the impact of this significant relationship on the rest of his life.

— Rachael Berg-Martinez, Ph.D., Licensed Clinical Psychologist

*Reading this book is the permission I needed to also
continue to "love the things I wish had not happened".
In a time when our mental and emotional health
is heavily judged and shamed, I am forever grateful for
the time Octavio spent to share his story so completely.*

— KAYLA GRACE TALBOT,

FOUNDER, THE EVERYDAY HUMAN

*Accounts of alcoholism, abuse and adultery are all
too common in contemporary American culture.
No matter how different the story, the result is the same:
rejection and hate. Octavio's story is a must read of
release and freedom, but most important, forgiveness.*

— Joe Vinatieri, Mayor, City of Whittier

Octavio engages the subject of forgiveness with raw honesty, humility and depth. He invites us into his suffering, struggle and ultimately, his freedom, without justification or candy-coating. If you have ever been hurt, betrayed or disappointed, this book is for you. If you have ever sought revenge, punished someone for their misdeeds or self-righteously judged another, this book is for you. In short, if you're human, this book is for you. It's emotional and spiritual CPR; breathe it in.

— Jean-Marie Jobs, President GAP community Inc., CEO yellow marker

These are clear words about how it feels being a boy, being a teenager and, being a wounded man who finally found his way to freedom. It is a wonderful story of how we can overcome what has darkened our lives for decades...

— Dr. Uli Marienfeld,
Study Director ESBZ Berlin

*This searing, open-hearted account is courageous
in its complexity and honesty. The seemingly impossible
journey of grief, acceptance, and forgiveness recorded
in this work is one shared, to some extent, by every one
of us. This book takes the often abstract concepts of
grace and compassion and makes them exquisitely—often
painfully—real. I am grateful to its author.*

— Jonathan Puls, M.F.A., M.A., Associate Dean,
Fine Arts and Communication

*A story of authentic pain that bruised my heart and
shed light to the pathway of freedom — forgiveness.*

— Neil Nakamoto, Chief Consultant,
KeyCoachng International; Project
Administrator: Jupiter Icy Moon
Orbiter Project, JPL, former

Like a glass of fresh water on a hot summer day,
this book will refresh your soul. It is liquid poetry that
you will want to drink in one sip. Octavio is
the real deal. He prepared a great refreshing drink
out of each word he wrote that will feed and imprint
hope in your soul. It is hot out there, just start
drinking away.

— Dr. Bruno Interlandi, Founder,
Never Too Late For You Ministries

This book is a must read, for anyone dealing with the "black holes caused by unseen wounds" and for those struggling to move forward despite the strong gravitational pull of past hurts. Thank you Octavio for being a great story teller and for inviting us into your personal journey.

— Adaumir Nascente, Director of Care Operations, Unitymedia, and Pastor, Mosaik Düsseldorf

I am grateful Octavio shared his story. The story is raw and redemptive. His story gives hope to others in a world where hope is a rare commodity.

—Eric Bryant, Pastor at Gateway Church, Author of Not Like Me: Learning to Love, Serve, and Influence Our Divided World

It Was a Beautiful Day When My Father Died will ask and nudge you to stop, turn around, and see those moments in your own life that are perhaps soul scenes you didn't even know were impacting you. It's a call to the reader to pause to consider the echoes of the past that find themselves in one's present life-song and future. What a read indeed!

—Dr. David Gonzalez, Jr., Assistant Professor of Public Administration & Organizational Leadership; American Society for Public Administration, member

*It Was a Beautiful Day When My Father Died is a
profound and timely story. In our bitterly divided, us
& them world, Octavio Martinez reminds us that
there is a better way: forgiveness. Moreover, Octavio's
ability to place the reader inside his world is uncanny.
He is a true storyteller. This book doesn't merely
recall a few stories from the past. No, it invites you to
feel what the author felt, to wrestle with your
own bitterness and pride, and to consider the power
of forgiveness. Read this book.*

— Kevin Knox, Author of NO MATTER WHAT;
    Former Pastor of Mosaic Bay Church

*Octavio writes with unfiltered honesty about the pain
of growing up with parental and self-inflicted
physical abuse. He shares with power and beauty
the meaning, reasons for, and steps toward embracing
the new life God intended through forgiveness.
Short but packed with human tragedy and victory,
this book is inspired reading giving hope to those with
scarred childhood memories.*

— Janice Sakuma, Mosaic, LA Leadership
    Team former

*Octavio's example and encouragement to forgive my
father led to an amazing breakthrough. Thank you
for being a voice of truth and wisdom at a time
when I desperately needed it. Thanks also for being a
friend and on top of that a great pastor.*

—Toby de la Torre, Flight Attendant

My hands are covered with scars and broken bones. They are the story of my anger, self-abuse, violence, and stupidity. Now, I want them to tell a different story. My first tattoo is on my fingers.